Roosevelt and Kennedy

Roosevelt and Kennedy

by John Ray

Senior Master,
The Hugh Christie School, Tonbridge

 HEINEMANN EDUCATIONAL BOOKS · LONDON

Heinemann Educational Books Ltd

LONDON EDINBURGH MELBOURNE TORONTO
AUCKLAND SINGAPORE JOHANNESBURG
HONG KONG NAIROBI IBADAN

SBN 435 31757 1

Published by Heinemann Educational Books Ltd
48 Charles Street, London W1X 8AH
Photoset in Malta by St Paul's Press Ltd
Printed in Great Britain by Morrison and Gibb Ltd
London and Edinburgh

Contents

Introduction

Among the presidents of the United States of America, two have been particularly outstanding during the 20th century. They were both Democrats and their lives have left their mark not only on their own country, but also on the rest of the world. Franklin D. Roosevelt and John F. Kennedy became world figures in their own lifetimes.

Both came from rich families which were closely involved in political life. Each had a determination to succeed and fought his way to the top. The two men had personal charm and were able to inspire loyalty from others. Physical courage is a quality to be admired and both presidents, especially Roosevelt, showed this in overcoming physical handicaps and carrying out their work.

During the years covered by this book the United States and Britain drew close in their aims and policies. In the 1930's aggressive dictatorship was a growing menace to both countries. In the Second World War, by 1941, they were fighting a common enemy. The crises that have arisen since the end of the war have affected the whole world and they have often been met by a joint action by the United States and Britain. Both these presidents were deeply concerned with this link with Britain.

The two men were involved in the Second World War. As President, F. D. Roosevelt carried a tremendous burden of responsibility towards his fellow countrymen, knowing that one wrong decision could sent thousands to their deaths. At the same time the young naval officer, J. F. Kennedy was learning the difficult art of leadership in action.

To understand the growth of the world's most powerful state, it is necessary to know something of the two men who held the supreme position in their country during some vital years. One died, worn out by the demands of work; the other was brutally murdered by a sniper's bullet. Both have left their mark on the story of mankind. Here, then are the stories of two men who made history.

Franklin D. Roosevelt

The Early Years

In the United States of America, an election for the Presidency takes place every four years. The election campaign is a great strain for the candidates. They have to travel hundreds of miles across the vast country, addressing dozens of meetings, shaking hands with thousands of people, and living in a bright glare of publicity. The office of President is a glittering prize for the winner, bringing world-wide fame and enormous power and responsibility.

Therefore, the achievement of becoming President four times in succession is an amazing performance. Indeed this record has been attained by only one American. What makes his story even more remarkable is the fact that he was a cripple, who had no power to use his legs. The man was Franklin Delano Roosevelt.

The Roosevelt family was descended from early Dutch settlers in America, dating from the 17th century. In the 19th century one of the descendants, James Roosevelt, was a businessman. He was rich and lived in comfortable surroundings. When he was 52 years old, in 1880, he married a distant cousin, Sara Delano, who was only half his age. At their home, on 30th January 1882, was born a son named Franklin Delano Roosevelt.

He was an only child and had a happy boyhood. His mother lavished care and affection on him all through her life. Franklin had nurses and governesses to look after him. The family travelled a great deal and the boy was taken to Europe on his first trip when he was only two years old. By the time that he had reached the age of 14 he had visited Europe eight times.

1. Sara Delano Roosevelt with her son Franklin.

As a boy, Franklin showed some signs of the leadership that he displayed later. His mother, Sara, commented on this:

Franklin had a great habit of ordering his playmates around, and for reasons which I have never been able to fathom was generally permitted to have his way. I know that I, overhearing him in conversation one day with a little boy on the place with whom he was digging a fort, said to him: 'My son, don't give the orders all the time. Let the other boy give them sometimes.' 'Mummie,' he said to me quite without guile, lifting a soil streaked face, 'if I don't give the orders nothing would happen.'[1]

The Roosevelts lived some time each year in a suite of of rooms at a New York hotel. On other occasions they stayed at their country home, which was on an island off the coast of New Brunswick. Franklin soon learned to sail and gained a love for the sea which he always kept. As James Roosevelt was President of the Louisville, New Albany and Chicago Railroad, he had his own private railway carriage in which the family travelled. It included a sitting room, a kitchen and bedrooms.

At the age of 14 the boy went to a famous school, Groton. There, the discipline was firm and life could be tough, the pupils getting up at 7 a.m. to take a cold shower. Franklin was happy and popular at school, where he stayed until 1900.

By that time the name of Roosevelt had become well known in America. A distant relation, Theodore Roosevelt, had become very successful in politics. 'Teddy' was an unusual man, very clever and an enthusiast in keeping fit. He had written books, worked on a ranch, and led a cavalry regiment in Cuba during the Spanish-American War of 1898. During the same year he became Governor of New York State and was then chosen as Vice-President of the U.S.A. in 1900. In September 1901 he succeeded to the Presidency when President William McKinley was assassinated. 'Teddy' Roosevelt was a character, full of zest and action, loved by many, but hated by others because of the showy way in which he conducted politics. When he was President, he often boxed with sparring partners, took lessons in jujitsu and went for long, hard cross-country walks.

2. Franklin Roosevelt at the age of six.

Franklin at this time was developing into a fine looking young man. He had great charm and a good voice. His father died at the end of 1900 and left considerable wealth to the family. Sara Roosevelt received most of it. But to Franklin there was left $100,000 which could be invested to bring a regular income. He went as a student to Harvard University, while his mother moved nearby to Boston.

During 1903 Franklin visited England. His easy-going American manner was used to overcome the very formal manners of the Edwardian Age which he found. In a letter to his mother he wrote:

I walked up to the best looking dame in the bunch and said 'Howdy?' Things at once went like oil and I was soon having flirtations with three of the nobility at the same time.[2]

Then, at the end of the year, he suddenly announced that he wanted to marry his cousin, Eleanor. She was from another branch of the Roosevelt family and was a niece of the famous President, 'Teddy'. Eleanor was 19 and a rather shy girl. She wrote later:

. . . without rhyme or reason I felt the urge to be part of the stream of life, and so in the autumn of 1903, when Franklin Roosevelt, my fifth cousin, once removed, asked me to marry him, though I was only nineteen, it seemed entirely natural and I never even thought that we were both young and in-experienced . . . my grandmother, when I told her, asked me if I was sure I was really in love. I solemnly answered 'yes', and yet I know now that it was years later before I understood what being in love or what loving really meant.[3]

The wedding in 1905 was a great social event attended by the President. The young couple were very rich, for Eleanor had inherited $100,000 from her father. Sara constantly provided money for them and soon lived with them. Children came along, first a girl, Anna, then boys. They were a happy family.

Having trained in law, Franklin worked in a lawyer's office. In politics he was a Democrat, unlike Teddy who was a Republican. When an opportunity came to enter political life in 1910, he took it and was elected as a state senator. Soon his good looks, fine voice and personal charm brought him promotion in the Party. He accepted the post of Assistant Secretary to the Navy in 1913. Roosevelt was obviously pleased with his personal success. But also there was the feeling that he could be of service to his country. Of the Roosevelt family he later wrote:

They have never felt that because they were born in a good position they could put their hands in their pockets and succeed. They have felt, rather, that, being born in a good position, there is no excuse for them if they do not do their duty by the community, and it is because this idea was instilled into them from birth that they have in nearly every case proved good citizens.[4]

Soon came the outbreak of the First World War. For some time the U.S.A. remained neutral, even though she disliked the submarine warfare which was waged by German U-boats. Tempers rose when the *Lusitania* was torpedoed off the Irish coast in 1915 and among the victims drowned were many American citizens. Then, in April 1917, war was declared. Roosevelt's life became busier as the U.S. Navy played an active part in ferrying men and materials across the Atlantic Ocean. He made a trip to Europe to visit the war zone.

When the Armistice came, Roosevelt attended the Versailles Conference as an observer. With his wife, he travelled back to the U.S.A. with President Wilson afterwards.

In 1920, Franklin was defeated in an election for the post of Vice-President. The Democrats were routed by the Republicans and he lost his position in the government. Therefore he returned to work as a lawyer, spending most of his time in New York.

Then came tragedy and a complete change in the lives of the Roosevelt family. They went, in 1921, for a holiday to

3

3. *Franklin Roosevelt in 1920 at the time of his resignation as Assistant Secretary for the Navy.*

Campobello, their island property. During August, after some vigorous exercise and swimming, Franklin became ill. At first it was thought that he had a severe chill. But then there came a time when he could not use his legs. His muscles could not move his limbs. Doctors soon realised that he had contracted infantile paralysis, the complaint which is known today as polio.

The Difficult Years

The blow to the family was enormous. A man full of energy, strength and personality, the father of young children, had been stricken down. His mind remained sharp, but his body was apparently useless. The shock to Roosevelt can be imagined; his dreams of success must have appeared to vanish. But he treated his misfortune with a typical courage. As his son James said:

The true greatness of F. D. R., the father, came about from the very beginning of his affliction, for even in those first terrible days, when the daggers were cutting deep into agonized muscle and flesh, he was grinning (though he clenched his teeth to do it), jesting and striving to pass it all off as a nothing, a nuisance, to ease the shock on the five scared kids who watched him.[5]

His wife, Eleanor, came to play an even more important part in the family life. She had to carry out many of the family duties that had been performed by the once active husband. But Roosevelt's spirit was tremendous. Over the next few years he refused to give in, making a supreme effort to regain his strength and movement. In a letter, written on 8th December 1922, he commented:

. . . The combination of warm weather, fresh air and swimming has done me a world of good; in fact, except for my legs I am in far better physical shape than ever before in my life, and I have developed a chest and a pair of shoulders on me which would make Jack Dempsey envious. The legs are really coming along finely, and when I am in swimming work perfectly. This shows that the muscles are all there, only require further strengthening. I am still on crutches but get about quite spryly, and, in fact, have resumed going to my office down town two or three times a week.[6]

Gradually, Franklin was able to take an increasingly active part in life. His legs were apparently useless. Yet leg irons were fitted and, when he used a stick, he was

4

able to take a few steps, leaning on someone's arm. He swam again, as this was one way in which he could achieve movement. 'The water put me where I am and the water will bring me back,' he said. The pain was sometimes great and the effort was tremendous. But Roosevelt was a man of unusual determination. It would have been easy to sit back and lead the life of a total cripple, removed from the world. Instead of that, he maintained an interest in his business and legal affairs. Also, he kept in touch with politics, being determined to make a return. People began to take notice of the courage of a man whose every movement was a physical exertion:

. . . the picture of a fight back from crippling illness was itself of vote-gathering importance. During his illness he sent three thousand letters annually to politicians to keep his contacts alive; his wife became reporter and runner, eyes and ears. The pursuit of power was calculated and self-conscious.[7]

In 1928 Roosevelt was persuaded to re-enter politics. His rich voice was heard again at meetings. He became a candidate for the Governorship of New York, a very important office. The contest was close, but Franklin was successful by about 25,000 votes. Over the whole country, however, there were Republican victories. The new President was Herbert Hoover.

From the end of the First World War, the U.S.A. had enjoyed a boom in trade. During the period 1914 to 1918 she had provided goods for the countries at war; she had captured some of their overseas markets; she had grown rich. When peace came, American industry expanded. She had enormous exports and much money was invested in a Europe that had suffered great damage and losses during the fighting.

It was a time of what was called Isolationism. America cut herself off from the rest of the world. She would not join the League of Nations. High tariffs – import taxes – were imposed on foreign goods. Therefore, while America grew more and more powerful, many other lands suffered. Because it was so difficult to sell to her, they could not repay the loans which she had made to them.

The Republicans were pleased with the prosperity that the 1920's brought to their land. The standards of living of millions of ordinary Americans rose. Mass production led to millions of goods becoming available on the market. Methods of hire-purchase enabled working people to buy them easily. Herbert Hoover, during a speech made in 1928, said:

. . . our American experiment in human welfare has yielded a degree of well-being unparalleled in all the world. It has come nearer to the abolition of poverty, to the abolition of fear of want, than humanity has ever reached before. Progress of the past seven years is the proof of it.[8]

This was the atmosphere of the country in which the Roosevelt family lived. For them, life was busy with a variety of happenings. Franklin wrote to a friend in 1929:

The family is going through the usual tribulations. James is getting over pneumonia; Elliott is about to have an operation; Franklin Jr has a double broken nose and John has just had a cartilage taken out of his knee! Anna and her husband . . . are taking a short holiday in Europe and their baby is parked with us at the Executive Mansion. Eleanor is teaching school two and a half days a week . . . So you see that it is a somewhat hectic life.[9]

Then, to this world, there came the Great Slump or Great Depression, which brought disaster to millions, yet brought Franklin Roosevelt to the Presidency of the United States. Today its causes are still not clearly understood. What happened was that the American trade boom suddenly came to an end. Instead of the massive buying of shares, people rushed to sell them. On 24th October 1929, about 13 million were sold; on 29th October, about 16 million changed hands. Shares lost their value. They

brought only a mere fraction of the price that had earlier been paid for them. Overnight, fortunes were lost. Companies became bankrupt. Factories had to close. Thousands of men and women became unemployed. A dreadful poverty struck the country which had known such prosperity only a short time before:

Families and entire communities were depressed to the verge of starvation; packs of men, women and children roamed the land looking for work and food; shanty towns constructed of cardboard and rubble rose on the outskirts of most cities . . . apple sellers appeared on the street corners of downtown New York offering apples for sale in the attempt to salve their pride by appearing not to beg; breadlines which sometimes stretched for entire city blocks queued at charity stations for relief; scavengers sorted the rubbish at city dumps looking for edible scraps.[10]

The trouble soon spread to Europe because much American money was invested there. In the world of modern trade, a depression in one country can soon affect others. Britain was badly hit and some of her older industries – coal mining, shipbuilding and cotton – suffered particularly.

5. *Unemployed men queuing for relief money in New York during the Great Depression.*

In America, the government made efforts to meet the crisis over the next years:

The statistics of this vast operation are overwhelming. Over 27,000 carloads of wheat, 30,000 of flour and 7,800 of stock-feed were shipped the length and breadth of the land. These supplies ultimately reached all but 17 of the 3,098 counties in the United States, and the result was the distribution of over 10,000,000 barrels of flour to 5,000,000 million families. In cotton distribution, 540,000 bales of finished garments, 211,000 of yard goods, and 92,000 blankets and comforters were handled. Approximately the same number of families as were given flour were the recipients of over 66,000,000 ready-made garments, 38,000,000 chapter-made garments, and 3,000,000 blankets.[11]

But in spite of these efforts, the terrible decline in trade continued. By 1932 the effects of the Great Depression were so great that almost 13 million Americans were unemployed. Some of them had lost all hope of recovery.

At this stage Roosevelt allowed his name to be considered as a possible Democratic Party candidate for the Presidency of the U.S.A. At the Party Convention, in Chicago, he was chosen.

Then came the strain of the election tour. His opponent was the Republican, Herbert Hoover. Roosevelt's message was plain. Millions of Americans needed work – he would offer them a New Deal. The Republicans had failed to take care of the country's 'Forgotten Men'. During a speech at Michigan on 2nd October 1932, he said:

. . . there are two theories of prosperity and of well-being; The first theory is that if we make the rich richer, somehow they will let a part of their prosperity trickle down to the rest of us. The second theory – and I suppose this goes back to the days of Noah – I won't say Adam and Eve, because they had a less complicated situation – but, at least, back in the days of the flood, there was the theory that if we make the average of mankind comfortable and secure, their prosperity will rise upward, just as yeast rises up, through the ranks.[12]

Roosevelt felt the urgency of the problem which was paralysing America. Government aid was not enough:

The country needs and, unless I mistake its temper, the country demands bold, persistent experimentation. It is common sense to take a method and try it. If it fails, admit it frankly and try another. But above all, try something.[13]

The election result was an overwhelming victory for Roosevelt. He went to Washington, a crippled President faced by the greatest financial disaster ever to strike any nation. By that time, 17 million of his countrymen were without work. But his strength of purpose did not waver. It was shown by one of his comments: 'If you have spent two years in bed trying to wiggle your big toe, everything else seems easy.'

At the Inauguration Ceremony on 4th March 1933, he took the oath. Article II, Section I of the Constitution of the U.S.A., says:

Before he enter on the execution of his office, he shall take the following oath or affirmation: 'I do solemnly swear (or affirm) that I will faithfully execute the office of President of the United States, and will to the best of my ability, preserve, protect and defend the Constitution of the United States.[14]

Then, in his Inaugural Address he showed determination. He, who came from a comfortable background and lived in wealthy surroundings, felt a great sympathy for the common man. Immediate effort was needed:

. . . This nation asks for action, and action now. Our greatest primary task is to put people to work. There is no unsolvable problem if we face it wisely and courageously.

It can be accomplished in part by direct recruiting by the government itself, treating the task as we would treat the emergency of a war . . .[15]

He decided to speak to the nation. The development of radio enabled him to speak to ordinary people. His 'Fireside Chats' became famous as he explained his policies to his countrymen. They were taken into his confidence. His wife, Eleanor, wrote:

His voice lent itself remarkably to the radio. It was a natural gift, for in his whole life he never had a lesson in diction or public speaking. His voice unquestionably helped him to make the people of the country feel that they were an intelligent and understanding part of every government undertaking during his administration.[16]

To meet the nation's problems Roosevelt introduced his 'New Deal'. He gathered around him a set of very able men to carry out the detailed work. They could see that the first essential was to offer work to the unemployed. If private

6. *The President and his family on the announcement of his second election victory.*

7. *Roosevelt delivering a 'fireside chat'.*

8. *The President opening the U.S. baseball season.*

enterprise could not do this, then the State would have to play a part. Therefore, the Federal government, that is the government of the U.S.A. in Washington, made loans to the government of each state. They in turn began schemes of employment. Projects were begun to build roads and construct bridges. Areas of land were planted with thousands of trees. By 1935 great steps had been taken to offer work to men whose spirit had been almost broken.

The best known scheme under the New Deal was the setting up of the Tennessee Valley Authority (T.V.A) in May 1932. As the map shows, it covered an area which included parts of seven separate states. Power plants and dams were constructed so that hydro-electric power could be used by a large area. Farmers were able to improve their methods. Electrically driven machinery helped them.

The Agricultural Adjustment Act aimed to maintain farm prices. Farmers were paid, in some cases, to destroy part of their crops and slaughter some of their animals. For example, 6 million pigs were killed to help keep up the price of pork.

By 1935 some progress had definitely been made. There were still unemployed but the American people generally appreciated the efforts made by Roosevelt in taking positive steps to meet the crisis. They respected a man who could achieve so much while he had to fight his own battle against his disability of not being able to walk. However, some Americans objected to the New Deal. Many felt that individual firms and people should work their own way out of economic trouble.

In 1936 there came the time for another Presidential election. Speaking before the Democratic State Convention, at Syracuse, New York, on 29th September, Roosevelt reminded his audience of the position which had faced the U.S.A. before the previous election:

In the spring of 1933 we faced a crisis which was the ugly fruit of twelve years of neglect . . . Do I need to recall to you the fear of those days – the reports of those who piled supplies

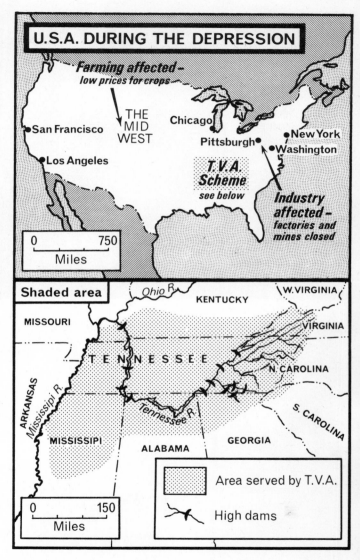

in their basements, who laid plans to get their fortunes across the border . . . Do I need to recall the law-abiding heads of peaceful families, who began to wonder, as they saw their children starve, how they would get the bread they saw in the bakery window . . .?[17]

When the voting returns were announced, Franklin Roosevelt had won the greatest election victory in all of America's history. Of the 48 states he gained 46. The Republican Party's candidate, Alfred Landon, suffered a crushing defeat.

Back in office, the work of the New Deal continued. During the period 1935–39 many of its laws were aimed at providing greater social security and more rights for working people. Insurance acts were passed. Cripples and blind people were helped. These were measures that appealed particularly to Roosevelt's ideals.

But he had many opponents. Republicans often accused him of seeking too much power and of taking away individual freedom. They said that government interference and schemes for social benefits took away initiative and were too much like communism. Also, some of his enemies disliked Roosevelt as a person. Commenting on this, Harold Ickes, the Secretary of the Interior said, in 1936:

It seems a quality of the Roosevelt character either to inspire a mad devotion that can see no flaw or to kindle a hatred of an intensity that will admit of no virtue . . . It may be taken for granted that he is neither saint nor devil, archangel nor foul fiend. A very human individual, he possesses faults as well as virtues.[18]

In the White House, life was always busy. Eleanor Roosevelt was completely involved in her husband's work, acting as hostess and giving him the assistance needed to cope with his many tasks. Here is an extract from *The Autobiography of Eleanor Roosevelt* which shows something of the duties of a President's wife:

I include here a sample of my social calendar for one week. I think you will see that a president's wife is not exactly idle.

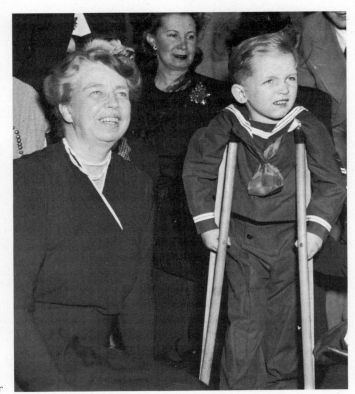

9. *Eleanor Roosevelt during a fund-raising party to help victims of infantile paralysis.*

Monday
1.00 p.m. Lunch with Mrs Hull
4.00 p.m. Tea for 175 guests
5.00 p.m. Tea for 236 guests

Tuesday
1.00 p.m. Lunch with Mrs Garner
4.00 p.m. Tea for members of Delaware Democratic Club
4.30 p.m. Tea for foreign diplomats' wives
7.00 p.m. Dinner for 22
9.00 p.m. Judicial reception

10. *Eleanor Roosevelt, King George VI, Sara Roosevelt, Queen Elizabeth, and Franklin Roosevelt.*

Wednesday
4.00 p.m. Tea for 266 guests
5.00 p.m. Tea for 256 guests

Thursday
1.00 p.m. Formal luncheon for 52 guests
*4.00 p.m. Tea, women's division of Infantile Paralysis
Foundation*
*5.00 p.m. Tea for Executive Board of the Federation of
Women's Clubs*

Friday
1.00 p.m. Lunch for wives of Cabinet members
*8.00 p.m. Diplomatic dinner – 94 guests
197 additional guests for music after dinner*[19]

Also, his mother, the former Sara Delano, took a keen interest in her son's progress. She was present in 1939 during the following incident. It occurred during the visit to the U.S.A. of King George VI and Queen Elizabeth:

Franklin had a tray of cocktails ready in front of him, and his mother sat on the other side of the fireplace looking disapprovingly at the cocktails and telling her son that the King would prefer tea. My husband, who could be as obstinate as his mother, kept his tray in readiness, however . . . As the King approached my husband and the cocktail table, my husband said, 'My mother does not approve of cocktails and thinks you should have a cup of tea'. The King answered, 'Neither does my mother', and took a cocktail.[20]

The Second World War

While the U.S.A. was taking steps to defeat the Great Slump and the Roosevelt family were busily engaged in many activities, the shadow of war was approaching in Europe. The Slump had caused massive unemployment there. In Britain, during 1932, there were almost 3 millions without work. Germany was worse hit, because so much American capital, invested there during the 1920's, was withdrawn when the financial crisis came. The German total of unemployed was about 6 millions. Therefore, a chance of power in Germany came to Adolf Hitler and his Nazi Party. Their dictatorship appeared to offer a way out of the Slump, promising work to the unemployed. They came to power in 1933.

From that year until 1939 the strength of dictatorship grew in several countries and an alliance of Germany, Italy and Japan appeared to offer a threat to the peace of the world. During the period, the U.S.A. was still strongly isolationist, not wishing to become involved in the affairs of countries overseas. But the peace was uneasy. Various acts of aggression made it obvious that war was approaching. For example, Italy attacked Abyssinia, Japan attacked China and Germany occupied Austria and Czechoslovakia.

Then in 1939 came war. Generally, the American people supported the efforts of the democracies, France and Britain, against the dictatorships. But they did not wish to be drawn into the conflict themselves. Roosevelt, however, realised that a clash would come in the long run. When the Germans obtained their great victories in 1940, only Great Britain stood between Hitler and a complete German triumph in Western Europe. Britain's leader was Winston Churchill, whose mother had been an American. He had always sought to maintain close links with the U.S.A. and he now asked for help. Materials of war – guns, ships, ammunition and aircraft were desperately needed.

In spite of the opposition of some of his countrymen, Roosevelt took steps to send assistance. For example, 50 old American destroyers were transferred to the Royal Navy. The President realised that the policy of giving help to Britain would bring protection to the U.S.A. also. Later, there followed the policy of 'Lend-Lease'. In a Fireside Chat on 29th December 1940 he said:

If Great Britain goes down, the Axis powers will control the continents of Europe, Asia, Africa, Australia and the high seas – and they will be in a position to bring enormous military and naval resources against this hemisphere...There is far less chance of the United States getting into the war if we do all we can now to support the nations defending themselves against the Axis...We must be the arsenal of democracy.[21]

The year 1940, apart from the dramatic events in world history, saw a remarkable milestone in Roosevelt's life. He decided to stand for a third term as the Democratic candidate in the Presidential election. No man previously had held the office for that period of time. After a hard election tour the people of the U.S.A. showed their confidence in the man who had helped to overcome the worst effects of the Great Slump and was now preparing them to guard democracy.

Back in office, the President addressed his Annual Message to Congress on 6th January 1941. Part of it was:

In the future days, which we seek to make secure, we look forward to a world founded upon four essential human freedoms:
The first is freedom of speech and expression – everywhere in the world.
The second is freedom of every person to worship God in his own way – everywhere in the world.
The third is freedom from want – which, translated into world

13

terms, means economic understandings which will secure to every nation a healthy peace-time life for its inhabitants – everywhere in the world.

The fourth is freedom from fear – which, translated into world terms, means a world-wide reduction of armaments to such a point and in such a thorough fashion that no nation will be in a position to commit an act of physical aggression against any neighbour – anywhere in the world.[22]

Later in the year, after Roosevelt and Churchill had met secretly, they issued the famous 'Atlantic Charter', which set out these ideals as the main hopes of the free world.

The war spread. In June 1941 Germany attacked Russia and won sweeping victories. It appeared that the whole of Europe was about to be swallowed by the dictators, Hitler and Mussolini. In the Far East, trouble was brewing. The Japanese, a most powerful race had attacked China. The U.S.A., as a Pacific naval power, was deeply interested in affairs in that area. She disliked the way in which the Japanese were waging the war against China. Talks were arranged at which the American and Japanese points of view could be put forward.

The Japanese realised that the forces of the U.S.A. in the Pacific stood as a barrier to their ideas of expansion. Therefore a plan was devised to strike a devastating blow against the American naval and air strength in that area. It was to be followed up by the rapid occupation of American, British and Dutch territories in that part of the world.

On 7th December 1941, out of the peaceful morning sky above the U.S. naval base at Pearl Harbor in the Hawaiian Islands, several hundred Japanese bombers and fighters appeared. They had been secretly flown from aircraft carriers. Their bombs and torpedoes sank seven of the eight battleships of the U.S. Pacific Fleet. With this terrible blow, the Japanese announced that war had begun. President Roosevelt was now at the head of a nation whose aim was to revenge the treachery and destroy dictatorship.

Winston Churchill visited the U.S.A. soon after Pearl Harbor. Speaking before both houses of Congress on 26th December 1941, he said:

It is not given to us to peer into the mysteries of the future. Still, I avow my hope and faith, sure and inviolate, that in the days to come, the British and American peoples will, for their own safety and for the good of all, walk together in majesty, in justice and in peace.[23]

America's determination was shown by Roosevelt. His country's power had been sorely hit by the Japanese. But the U.S.A. had more resources to call on than any other of the world's nations. She would hit back. In his message to Congress in January 1942 he said:

We cannot wage this war in a defensive spirit. As our power and our defences are fully mobilised, we shall carry the attack against the enemy – we shall hit him and hit him again wherever and whenever we can reach him.[24]

But at first the Japanese had tremendous successes. Within a short time, they had conquered Malaya, captured Singapore, taken Sumatra, Borneo, the Philippines and much of New Guinea. They even threatened the northern coasts of Australia. Their overwhelming strength, combined with their intelligent use of air/naval co-operation brought them many victories.

In May and June 1942, the President and his people were heartened by successes. In the former month there occurred the Battle of the Coral Sea, while in the latter was the Battle of Midway Island. They were both fought mainly by carrier-based aircraft so that fleets attacked each other without ever coming into gun range. Both were American victories and halted the Japanese advance.

Then the strength of America's industries began to show. Thousands of aircraft were built, scores of ships were launched and millions of tons of equipment were produced. Gradually the tide of war turned. American forces, supported by their allies, began to drive the

11. Crippled American warships at Pearl Harbor.

Japanese back towards their homeland. The operation was often costly. To remove enemy forces from their island strongholds cost the lives of thousands of men.

The war was a terrible strain on the President. Bearing in mind the physical effort needed to move, his activities were incredible, for he was no longer a young man. His mother Sara Delano Roosevelt, had died in 1941, at the age of eighty-six. Eleanor was still a support, but the responsibility of guiding the country's policies left their mark on him. For example, in 1943 he met Winston Churchill at Casablanca, in North Africa, for a conference, then he had visited South America before going to Cairo, in Egypt, then on to another conference with Churchill and Stalin at Teheran, in Persia.

As the Allied forces, in 1944, drove home their attacks, the Axis armies began to crumble. Both in Europe and in the Far East, victory was in sight. The question then arose of the President's future. Would he resign? Roosevelt surprised many Americans when he announced that he was willing to stand again. For a fourth time, at the end of

12. The Big Three at Yalta – Churchill, Roosevelt and Stalin.

the year, he went through an election campaign. He was elected by a very substantial majority.

But the President's days were numbered. His health was failing. Early in 1945 he made a long journey to Yalta, in the Crimea. There he had a conference with Stalin and Winston Churchill. The fighting in Europe was nearing its end and they made plans for the settlement of various parts of the world after the war.

Roosevelt had worked hard for the idea of setting up an organisation for maintaining peace – a United Nations Organisation. He was due to attend its opening on 25th April. Before this, however, he went for a short holiday to Warm Springs, Georgia. It was a much needed rest. Within a few months he had lost 36 pounds in weight and looked very ill. His wife remained in Washington.

On 12th April he sat for his portrait to be painted, just before lunch:

Suddenly the President groaned and slapped his left hand to his temple as if swatting a fly. He pressed hard and rubbed the spot. 'I have a terrific headache,' he said. Then he fell backward in the chair. Secret Service men carried him to the bedroom . . .[25]

He had suffered a brain haemorrhage. The news was given to Eleanor, back in Washington:

. . . I was called to the telephone. Steve Early, very much upset, asked me to come home at once. I did not even ask why. I knew that something dreadful had happened . . .

I got into the car and sat with clenched hands all the way to the White House. In my heart I knew what had happened, but one does not actually formulate these terrible thoughts until they are spoken. I went into my sitting room and Steve Early and Dr McIntyre came to tell me the news.[26]

13. *Roosevelt towards the end of his life, clearly showing the strain of wartime leadership.*

Franklin D. Roosevelt's death was mourned over the whole of the free world. A few months later there came the victory over dictatorship that he had worked for. He was buried in the rose garden at Hyde Park, Spring-wood, his birthplace and family home.

John F. Kennedy

Years of Preparation

Two shots from a sniper's rifle ended the life of one of the world's most famous and promising statesmen in 1963. John Fitzgerald Kennedy had already made a considerable name in international politics. He was generally popular and respected. Then, in a flash his life was snuffed out in a tragedy which horrified and saddened people everywhere.

The Kennedy family have lived in America for over a hundred years. Like many people in the U.S.A. they are of Irish extraction. Many Irish families are found on the eastern seaboard. There is an historical background and explanation for this.

During the 19th century the whole of Ireland was part of the United Kingdom. At that time, southern Ireland, Eire, did not exist as a separate state. Many Irishmen wished for independence from the rest of Great Britain and Home Rule for themselves so that they could have their own government. But much land in Ireland was owned by English landlords. All through the century the Irish were struggling for a better way of life and greater political rights.

In the 1840's Ireland suffered from a period of great depression and famine with the result that thousands of Irishmen left their homeland. They emigrated with their families to the United States. They hoped to find a better life there. Amongst these migrants were the Kennedys. Here was the start of their association with America.

Most Irish peasants in the last century existed on a diet of potatoes. It was an easy crop to grow on their smallholdings and provided them with a filling diet. In 1846 almost the whole crop was attacked by potato blight. What followed was a national tragedy. Many families faced starvation. Gradually, whole areas of the country were affected by the lack of food. Today, in the 20th century, governments make great and rapid efforts to overcome such emergencies. But little was done to meet the terrible situation. It was a time when the State felt little sense of duty towards its more unfortunate citizens: A visitor to a village in Ireland said:

Out of a population of 240, I found 13 already dead from want. The survivors were like walking skeletons; the men stamped with the living mark of hunger; the children crying with pain; the women in some of the cabins too weak to stand. When there before, I had seen cows at almost every cabin, and there were, besides, many sheep and pigs owned in the village. But now all the sheep were gone; only one pig left; the very dogs which had barked at me before had disappeared; no potatoes, no oats. We ordered a ton of meal to be sent there.[1]

President Kennedy's great-grand-father was named Pat Kennedy. He lived at that time in a small cottage at New Ross, in County Wexford. He decided to make the long and sometimes dangerous sea passage to the New World. After some time Pat Kennedy found a job as a cooper in Boston, Massachusetts. As the family settled, they became more successful.

Pat's son improved his position and succeeded him in business. He became owner of a wine and spirit firm and also owned two drinking saloons. In addition he was a partner in a coal company.

Pat's grandson, Joe Kennedy did well at school. He showed great promise in his lessons and had a sharp mind and great ability. In 1908 he left school and went to one of America's oldest and most famous universities – Harvard. There he studied economics. He realised that he had the will to succeed in the world of business. It is said that he determined to make a fortune of one million dollars for himself by the time that he was 35 years of age.

After leaving college he entered a bank and soon showed his capability for making progress. After borrowing some money he bought a small bank and thus became, at the age of 25, the youngest president of a bank in the U.S.A.

At that time he sought the hand of Rose Fitzgerald in marriage. She was the daughter of the mayor of Boston, the famous 'Honey Fitz'. There was some opposition to the proposed marriage because some people felt that Kennedy was not good enough for the young woman, as his family did not have a suitable background. But Joe Kennedy persevered. The wedding, which was a grand occasion took place on 7th October 1914. The young couple took a house in Brookline, a suburb of Boston.

Joe Kennedy's business success continued. The years after the First World War were a boom time in the U.S.A. and trade flourished. He began to invest money in buying cinemas. Soon he had bought about 30. Going to see films was becoming a popular form of entertainment in America at that time. Therefore Kennedy started to build himself a fortune.

Soon, the Kennedys had a family. The first child was named Joe. Then on 29th May 1917 the future President was born. He was christened John Fitzgerald, but was known to the family as Jack. Later, seven more children were born. They were Rosemary, Kathleen, Eunice, Patricia, Jean, Robert and Edward. Any study of President

Kennedy must take into account the strong loyalty felt by members of the family towards each other. At all times, brothers and sisters have supported the family's efforts. Joseph Kennedy later wrote:

All of them have always seemed to have a lot of fun and enjoyment out of being with each other, more so than you find in most big families. You hear a lot today about togetherness. Long before it became a slogan, I guess we had it.[2]

As Joe Kennedy's wealth increased he decided to move to New York. In the first place it was a great centre of business and finance. Secondly he found an amount of religious discrimination in Boston. He was a Roman Catholic and was disliked by some Protestants for that reason.

In New York the Kennedys moved first to Riverdale, then to a large house at Bronxville. A large and growing family meant much work for Mrs Kennedy and she gave careful attention to their upbringing. Religion played an important part in their lives and they were all carefully instructed in the Roman Catholic faith.

Joe Kennedy's business sense brought great success. With his wealth he was able to provide much comfort for his family. He bought a holiday home in Florida, at the famous Palm Beach. Another one which he purchased was at Cape Cod, in a place named Hyannisport. In the bay there, the two elder boys learned to sail small yachts. Jack Kennedy began a love for the sea which lasted all through his life.

He went to school in New York when he was young, then at the age of 13 left his home in New York to become a boarder at a Catholic preparatory school named Canterbury School, in Connecticut. He enjoyed sports such as baseball and American football. Also he became a keen swimmer. His classwork was not particularly good and his spelling was rather weak. At Easter 1931 he suddenly fell ill with an attack of appendicitis. When he had recovered, his parents decided to send him to another school.

The one chosen was Choate. His elder brother, Joe, was already there. The school was at Wallingford, Connecticut and was set in beautiful surroundings. He stayed there until he was 18.

Jack Kennedy was not the perfect pupil. After some time there his headmaster wrote to the boy's father. Part of the account said:

. . . he is casual and disorderly in almost all of his organisation projects. Jack studies at the last minute, keeps appointments late, has little sense of material values, and can seldom locate his possessions.[3]

Joe Kennedy always maintained a keen interest in his son's education, although his business commitments kept him very busy. The quality of Jack's work was average. His father urged him to make great efforts to succeed. In a letter to the boy, he wrote:

Now, Jack, I don't want to give the impression that I am a nagger, for goodness knows I think that is the worst thing any parent can be. After long experience in sizing up people I definitely know you have the goods and you can go a long way . . . I am not expecting too much and I will not be disappointed if you don't turn out to be a real genius, but I think you can be a really worthwhile citizen with good judgement and good understanding.[4]

Jack Kennedy realised that he had to work hard and sometimes regretted that he was not achieving more success. However, when he felt that he needed a larger allowance of pocket money he did not hesitate to write to his father, asking for it:

My recent allowance is 40¢. This I used for aeroplanes and other playthings of childhood but now I am a scout and I put away my childish things. Before I would spend 20¢ of my 40¢ allowance and in five minutes I would have empty pockets and nothing to gain and 20¢ to lose. When I am a scout I have to buy canteens, haversacks, blankets, searchlicgs poncho things

15. The Kennedy family. Seated left is Joseph Kennedy; behind him is John F. Kennedy aged 20. Robert Kennedy is leaning on the fireplace and Edward Kennedy is seated at his mother's feet.

that will last for years and I can always use it while I can't use chocolate marshmallow sunday ice cream and so I put in my plea for a raise of thirty cents for me to buy scout things and pay my own way around . . . [5]

At the age of 18 he left school. He intended to go to Princeton University, but first, to travel to England. There he was to spend a short time studying at the London School of Economics. However, as soon as he arrived in London he fell ill with an attack of jaundice. The illness held up his studies for some time. He entered Princeton University late, then was not well enough to maintain his studies there. At length he left, and in the autumn of 1936 went to Harvard University which is situated in Boston, where the family had started from.

His course of study was economics, history, English and French. Kennedy had always had a liking for history as a subject. He had read widely about the past. But his work at university did not reach a very high standard. His examination marks were rather poor.

However, he took a great and active interest in sport. There was plenty of opportunity to take part in games of American football and to go swimming. While playing football Jack Kennedy suffered a mishap which had a physical effect on him for the remainder of his life. The game is something like rugby football in Britain. During a match he injured his back. Often he was troubled by this ailment which affected his walking and standing. Nevertheless, he kept up some activity. He gained great pleasure from swimming and became very proficient at it, taking part in competitions.

During the summer of 1937 Kennedy visited Europe. He saw, at first hand, something of the troubles of European politics at that time. While visiting Italy he was able to meet the Pope. In that country he saw the Fascist regime of Mussolini at work. It was an example of dictatorship. Then, in Spain, he visited a country which was being torn by a terrible civil war. Europe was beginning the progress of violence which led to the outbreak of the Second World War in 1939.

Kennedy's interest in international affairs developed. He had lived in a family where politics was often a topic for discussion. But now he was able to see things more broadly. His travel was a most useful part of his education.

In 1937 a very important event occurred in the story of the Kennedy family. A replacement was needed for the American Ambassador to Britain. The President of the United States was Franklin D. Roosevelt. The man he appointed was Joe Kennedy. This was a remarkable change in fortune. Less than a century before, Pat Kennedy had left Ireland, which was then a part of Great Britain, as a poor man. Now his grandson returned to a great city, London, as the representative of one of the world's most powerful nations.

While his father came to London, Jack Kennedy was still at Harvard. In his third year there he made great progress. His elder brother, Joe, was at Harvard Law School. The two young men were able to meet each other often.

In Europe the international situation grew worse. Germany grew more powerful under the leadership of Adolf Hitler. During 1938 he made two extensions of his country's power. The first was the Anschluss, or union of Austria with Germany. Then, in the late summer, he made demands upon Czechoslovakia. The events there resulted in the Munich Crisis in which other European countries, especially Britain and France gave way to the Nazi leader's demands. But for a while, war had threatened.

What was America's attitude to these events? There was a strong feeling of Isolationism. Many Americans felt that what happened in other parts of the world was no concern of theirs. Europe was four or five day's journey away by ship. They did not wish to become involved in the affairs of foreign nations. Joe Kennedy, America's Ambassador in London, agreed with these opinions.

In the spring of 1939 Jack Kennedy came to London again. He travelled widely throughout the continent. The fact that his father was an ambassador helped him. He visited France, Poland, Russia, the Middle East and some of the countries of south-eastern Europe. It was useful for him, as a student of international affairs, to be in an area where the final steps towards war were being taken. On 1st September, Hitler's divisions crossed the Polish border and attacked that country. On 3rd September, Britain declared war on Germany. At that time Jack Kennedy was preparing to return to the U.S.A.

A Rising Politician

He worked hard during his last year at Harvard, having become deeply interested in politics, history and economics. As part of his study Kennedy wrote a long essay, or thesis on the subject of appeasement and the Munich Conference. In a capable piece of work he described the growth of German power and the way in which the democracies had done little to oppose Hitler's demands. He gained a good degree. His time at Harvard finished in 1940 and in July his first book was published. It was really a re-writing of his thesis and was entitled *Why England Slept*. The book warned America of the dangers which followed from not being prepared:

To say that democracy has been awakened by the events of the last few weeks is not enough. Any person will awaken when the house is burning down. What we need is an armed guard that will wake up when the fire first starts or, better yet, one that will not permit a fire to start at all.
We should profit by the lesson of England and make our democracy work . . .[6]

The publication of the book came at a perilous time in Britain's history. German armies had swept over Western Europe. Holland, Belgium and France collapsed before their onslaught. The British Expeditionary Force had been pressed back to Dunkirk, then evacuated by the Royal Navy. Britain stood alone against a vast and powerful enemy who controlled the European coastline from the North Cape down to the Spanish frontier. There followed the Battle of Britain, when the Germans attempted to smash the Royal Air Force before launching 'Operation Sealion'. This was to be the invasion of Britain.

In those difficult days Winston Churchill became Prime Minister. He sought the help of the U.S.A. in meeting a deadly enemy. But America remained Isolationist. Joe Kennedy, her Ambassador in London felt that the policy was right. And he also believed that Britain did not have the strength to stand up to German power. His views, when known, made him very unpopular. At the end of 1940 he resigned and returned to the U.S.A.

During those months, Jack Kennedy was undergoing a course of business studies in the U.S.A. In the early part of 1941 he tried to join the U.S. Army. However, his old

back injury troubled him and he was not accepted. He began to have exercises to strengthen his back and then in September enlisted in the U.S. Navy.

At first his work was routine. Kennedy's tasks involved Intelligence work for the Chief of Staff. But soon an event occurred which caused him to seek active service at sea. On 7th December 1941 came the Japanese attack on Pearl

16. *John Kennedy (*far right*) with the crew of PT 109.*

Harbor. In one stroke the Japanese devastated the power of the American Pacific Fleet. The U.S.A. was hurtled into war. It was some time, however, before Kennedy's request was granted. Through his father's influence he was posted, late in 1942. His destination was a motor torpedo boat squadron.

For some months he was on a training course in the

23

U.S.A. Jack Kennedy learned how to handle these craft. They call for skilful seamanship. Torpedo boats have highly powered engines which enable them to race across the sea at high speed. But because they are built for speed they are lightly constructed, with little armour plating. Therefore, in battle they are vulnerable to hits from shells, or even heavy machine-gun fire. The torpedo boat must race towards a larger, more powerfully equipped enemy in order to inflict damage. Then it releases its 'silver fish', torpedoes which cut through the sea at 40 or 50 m.p.h. before crashing into the enemy's side. One torpedo hit can sink a large ship. But while the torpedo boat is speeding into range a hail of fire is directed towards it. Kennedy, who had gained sailing skill at Hyannisport as a boy, passed the course well.

By the beginning of 1943 the Japanese advance in the Pacific area had been halted. America, who had been badly hit in the early months of the war built up her strength and struck back. At that point Kennedy was posted to the Solomon Islands and was given command of a small craft – *Patrol Boat 109*.

On 2nd August 1943 an event occurred which showed Jack Kennedy's courage and determination at their best, although it almost cost him his life. His vessel was patrolling an area called Blackett Strait and all seemed to be peaceful. Then in the dead of night, a Japanese destroyer came towards the torpedo boat at speed. There was hardly time to move before the enemy ship, the *Amagiri* cut the *P.T. 109* in half and sped on into the darkness.

Kennedy was flung across the boat. Half of it remained afloat, with the young skipper fortunately on board. He jumped into the sea and helped two other men towards the wrecked vessel. At length there were eleven sailors on the drifting wreck. Their position was precarious. Enemy forces were in the area and there seemed to be every chance that the survivors would be seen by them.

After some hours, what was left of *P.T. 109* sank. Kennedy and his men swam towards an island about three miles away. His early practice in swimming came to his aid.

He towed one wounded man by his life jacket and the journey took five hours. Although they managed to reach land they were not yet saved.

Kennedy showed leadership and bravery. After a rest he swam out for hours looking for help. None came. He then led his men towards Ferguson Passage where he hoped that a passing American vessel would sight them. He swam with another sailor to an island and managed to find some water and hard biscuits which had been left there. At length he came across some friendly natives who took him to a patrol of New Zealand soldiers. Then help was obtained for the remainder of his men.

During the whole operation, Kennedy showed bravery in leading his men. And he had a tenacity, a spirit of never giving in which was to be seen again later in his political life. For his courage, Kennedy was awarded a high decoration by the U.S. Navy:

His courage, endurance and excellent leadership contributed to the saving of several lives, and was in keeping with the highest tradition of the United States Naval Service.[7]

Kennedy stayed in the Pacific area until the end of 1943. He then returned to America, where he needed hospital treatment. This he obtained in a naval hospital at Boston. At that stage of the war tragedy came to the Kennedy family. It was the first stroke of an ill-fate which has dogged them ever since. First, the eldest brother, Joe was killed when his plane blew up during a bombing mission over Europe. Secondly, the husband of his sister, Kathleen, was killed in action.

Jack Kennedy was discharged from the U.S. Navy early in 1945. He had to plan for his future. There was no shortage of money in such a wealthy family. Joe Kennedy had set up a trust fund of one million dollars for each of his children when they reached the age of twenty-one. But the sons and daughters had been trained to use all of their abilities. At first he tried journalism, but after a short time gave it up. Then he decided on an attempt to enter the sphere of life where he was to achieve lasting success. This was politics.

The Kennedys were Democrats. Jack Kennedy set himself the ambition of achieving success in what is known to be a tough and competitive career. When a chance came of contesting a place in Congress he took the opportunity. First, there was an election to select a candidate to represent the Democratic Party. He launched into a campaign, determined to win this.

The area chosen was a part of Boston, Massachusetts, which was well known to the Kennedys. Jack toured the area, meeting and talking with hundreds of people. He soon learned the importance of discussing the problems of ordinary citizens, upon whom he would have to depend for support. His family helped him with their efforts and their great wealth. When the results of the campaign were announced many people were surprised to find that the young man had been easily successful. When the main election came along, Kennedy the Democrat, defeated the Republican candidate. At the age of 29 he had won a seat to Congress.

He often looked strangely out of place when he went to Washington. Other Congressmen were older in appearance and outlook. Kennedy was boyish and looked younger than his actual years. In the House of Representatives some Congressmen felt that he was too inexperienced to serve usefully.

Gradually, he built up a knowledge of practical politics. At first he listened attentively to other speakers and learned how to weigh up the value of their arguments. Then he began to take part in some debates. He became interested in trade unions. Also he gave his attention to debates on education.

Kennedy also came to show more concern for foreign affairs. In 1951 he travelled widely, first to Europe, then round the world, especially to the Far East. He was able to see for himself the building up of tension that the Cold War, that is the political argument between East and West, was bringing.

Kennedy had ambition. He decided that he wished to

17. The young Senator Kennedy with his wife in 1955.

25

become a Senator. Each American state returns two members to the Senate, which is a powerful section of America's government. Therefore, in 1952 the young Congressman stood for election in Massachusetts, a state which he knew well. With a typical thoroughness, which he showed again and again in political life, he began his campaign long before the voting took place. During 1949 and 1950 he travelled widely in the state, visiting scores of villages, towns and cities. Thousands of people came to hear of him as he shook hands, gave lectures, took part in debates and discussed matters with ordinary citizens in the streets. The great wealth of the Kennedy family enabled him to employ some excellent helpers and advisers to carry out the campaign.

His opponent was a widely respected man – Henry Cabot Lodge. He was a Republican and was already one of the two representatives from Massachusetts in the Senate. It appeared that Kennedy would have little chance of beating him. But when the voting returns came in it was seen that the high-pressure campaigning had had its effect. Over the whole country there was a swing towards the Republicans. But in Massachusetts, Kennedy defeated Cabot Lodge by a very small margin. At the age of 35 he became a Senator.

The following year, 1953, was important in Kennedy's life. For some time he had been considered a very eligible young bachelor, having a promising career ahead of him and possessing considerable wealth. At this time he was beginning to show a particular interest in one girl. Her name was Jacqueline Bouvier. She came from a rich family and worked as a photographer and reporter for the *Times-Herald* newspaper in Washington, as the 'Inquiring Camera Girl'. They became engaged in June and their wedding took place in September. It excited a great deal of public attention.

In his early days as Senator, Kennedy was faced with two particular difficulties. One was that he suffered at times from bad health. His old back injury caused him much trouble during 1954. Often he found walking very difficult

and tried many cures in an attempt to overcome the disability.

The other trouble was the activity of Senator McCarthy. He led large scale investigations in an attempt to find which Americans who were in positions of responsibility, had been connected with the Communist movement. Often his questions led to searching attacks, which were made unfairly, into peoples' lives. Kennedy was unsure of how much support to give him. Like McCarthy he disliked Communists, but he did not approve of McCarthy's methods.

At the end of the year a vote of censure was passed against McCarthy. Kennedy was in hospital when this happened. But because he had not come out openly against McCarthy's methods, Kennedy was blamed by some people for a long time after the incident was over.

His hospital visit was to enable an operation to be carried out. It was long, complicated and designed to relieve his pain. He became extremely ill and it looked as if his political life would suffer a severe setback. But his fighting spirit enabled him to make a rapid start towards recovery.

He began to write a book. As he convalesced it kept his mind occupied. The book was called *Profiles of Courage* and examined the lives of some famous Americans who had shown great courage in political life. When it was published in 1956 the work was a great success and brought more fame to the rising politician.

A Statesman of the World

When he returned to his work as Senator, Kennedy soon became known in many parts of the U.S.A. In 1956 a Presidential election was held and he decided to make a bid to gain the Democratic Party's nomination as Vice-President. Each party holds a convention, or large meeting before the election. There they vote to choose candidates who will attempt to become President and Vice-President. Kennedy was young by political standards. He was 39 years of age. But his 'team' of secretaries, public-relations men and helpers went into action. They organised a large campaign to encourage people to support their man. Kennedy lost the nomination to Senator Kefauver, but the whole campaign had given him more national publicity.

He continued to build up his experience of political matters. Foreign affairs interested him and his opinions gained more and more respect from those who heard them. He interested himself in matters within America, too. His policies generally were 'middle of the road'. This means that they did not swing to violent extremes. Thus he gained the reputation of being a moderate man and received support. There was, however, one matter of argument over Kennedy's position. He was a Roman Catholic and some people objected to this. They felt that his loyalty to his Church might come into conflict with his loyalty to his country. But Kennedy answered them:

My faith is a personal matter, and it doesn't seem to be conceivable, in fact it is impossible, that my obligation as one sworn to defend and uphold the Constitution could be changed by anything the Pope could say or do. What church I go to on Sunday, what dogma of the Catholic Church I believe in is my business, and whatever faith any other American has is his.[8]

During 1959, Kennedy decided to stand for the Presidency in the following year. He travelled all over the U.S.A., sometimes in his own aircraft, to seek support. First he had to be chosen by his own Party, the Democrats, as their representative. At their Convention, held in July 1960, he had an overwhelming victory over Adlai Stevenson, who had hoped to be chosen. Kennedy then picked his 'running-mate' to stand for the Vice-Presidency. He selected Lyndon B. Johnson the leader of the Democrats in the Senate.

In his acceptance address he said:

. . . We stand today on the edge of a new frontier – the frontier

18. *The Kennedys campaigning for the Presidency in New York.*

27

19. The victorious
Kennedy and the defeated
Richard Nixon after the
1960 election.

*of the 1960's – a frontier of unknown opportunities and perils –
a frontier of unfulfilled hopes and threats.*
*Woodrow Wilson's New Freedom promised our nation a new
political and economic framework. Franklin Roosevelt's New
Deal promised security and succour to those in need. But the
New Frontier of which I speak is not a set of promises – it is a
set of challenges. It sums up not what I intend to offer the
American people, but what I intend to ask of them. It appeals
to their pride, not their pocketbook . . .* [9]

The Republicans picked Richard Nixon as their candidate. For the two previous terms he had been Vice-
President, so was well experienced in all aspects of politics.

The 1960 election campaign was remarkable for the way
in which television brought the contest right into peoples'
homes. In particular, there were four debates between the

candidates when each was able to explain his proposed
policies. Kennedy had been given good practice and help
by his assistants in the methods of using television inter-
views to the best advantage. His appearances were a great
success.

Election day was held on 8th November 1960. The contest was extremely close and Kennedy's majority was very
small, out of 68 million votes which had been cast. At the
age of 43 he became America's youngest President ever. He
had reached the summit of ambition.

There began a period of great activity in American
history. Kennedy's time in office is often referred to as 'The
Thousand Days'. In that time a number of important events
occurred, both at home and abroad. Kennedy, like Roosevelt, planned a series of reforms which would improve the
position of the under privileged sections of American

20. *The President and his wife after his inauguration in 1961.*

21. *The President with John junior.*

society. He wanted to improve housing and social welfare for the poor, give equal rights to the Negroes and Puerto Ricans. He also saw it as America's responsibility to give aid and technical advice to the less well developed nations in South America, Africa and Asia.

In fact he was not able to carry through many of these reforms. This was partly because his period in office was so short but partly also because, like Roosevelt, he found a good deal of opposition in America. The Republicans opposed his legislation, and in this they had the support of the more conservative Democrats in Congress, especially those from the Southern States of America.

To help him carry the burdens of Presidency, Jacqueline Kennedy played an important part. She was an attractive, dignified woman who brought an air of elegance to life in the White House. In 1960 a son was born to the Kennedys.

He was named John and was a brother to Caroline who had been born in 1957. The President took great delight in his children. They brought a feeling of homeliness, even when important visitors from overseas were present, or when vital conferences were taking place. Jacqueline Kennedy supported her husband loyally, in all his ventures, accompanying him on many political trips and taking part in the large business of entertaining guests to the White House.

Kennedy gathered together a very able team of administrators round him. He was always ready to listen to a man talk upon a subject which the speaker thoroughly understood. The President could draw the best from people, inspiring them with his high hopes for the future of his country. As always, the Kennedy family gave much support. His younger brother, Robert, became Attorney-General in the government and used his skill in attempting to deal with many of America's problems. His father and mother were immensely proud of their son's achievements. But Joe Kennedy realised the President's burdens:

Jack doesn't belong any more to just a family. He belongs to the country. That's probably the saddest thing about all this. The family can be there. But there is not much they can do sometimes for the President of the United States. I am more aware now that I've ever been of the terrific problems that this country faces. In 1932 we only faced an economic problem. Now we face an economic problem, a farm problem, a defense problem – there isn't one phase of government that isn't faced with an immense problem. [10]

Soon after he came to office, Kennedy was faced with trouble very close to the U.S.A. There had been a revolution previously on the island of Cuba and Fidel Castro seized control. He had no love for the U.S.A. and was much more friendly, both in words and ideas, towards Russia and the Communist world. Some Cubans who had fled from their island to settle in the United States decided to launch a counter-invasion of Cuba. They wished to overthrow Castro.

They were given some help and encouragement by certain people in the U.S.A. including the U.S. Central Intelligence Agency, and when the small scale invasion took place at the Bay of Pigs in Cuba, it seemed that the government of the United States wanted it to succeed. In fact, it failed miserably. The invaders were quickly and easily rounded up. Naturally, much blame was attached to the President. Some said that he should never have allowed the invasion to begin. Others said that he should never have allowed it to fail. In any case it was a blow to American prestige in the Cold War.

Throughout the period since 1945, one of the World's greatest problems has been the Cold War, between the Communist and non-Communist nations of the world. In particular there has been intense rivalry between the U.S.S.R. and the U.S.A. The Russian leader, Nikita Kruschev, and the President of the United States met in June 1961 to attempt to settle some of the differences between their nations. The meeting took place in Vienna. Both men spoke their intentions clearly and forcefully. But the problems of the world could not be solved at one meeting.

A difficult period followed. In August, the Communists built a wall across Berlin, shutting off West Berlin from the rest of the city. West Berlin had been occupied by the Allies – Britain, France and the U.S.A. since the end of the Second World War. This was an attempt by the Communists to drive the western Allies out. The situation grew bad, but Kennedy led the determination of the Americans to stand fast.

The President also had to meet trouble within the United States. A point of great argument was the rights of Negroes. Their ancestors had been taken to the New World as slaves. After the end of the American Civil war in 1865 they were given their freedom. But they have never achieved equality with white people. Over recent years there has been a grow-

22. Race hatred: A National Guard holds back white Americans demonstrating against equal rights for Negroes.

ing movement to give them equal rights and opportunities. Although a number of Americans, especially those in the Southern states, felt that Kennedy was weak in giving way to these demands, the President stated his views clearly. By the time of his death the matter was still the cause of great argument within the U.S.A.:

... It ought to be possible for every American to enjoy the privileges of being an American without regard to his race or colour ... to have the right to be treated as he would wish to be treated, as one would wish his children to be treated ... This nation, for all its hopes and all its boasts, will not be fully free until all its citizens are free.[11]

In a television broadcast made to the American people on 11th June 1963 he said:

We preach freedom around the world, and we mean it, and we cherish our freedom here at home; but are we to say to the world and, much more importantly, to each other that this is a land of the free except for the Negroes; that we have no second-class citizens except Negroes; that we have no class or caste system, no ghettos, no master race except with respect to Negroes?[12]

At the end of 1962 there occurred the greatest crisis of the Kennedy administration. Again it involved Cuba. Finding

31

OXIDIZER VEHICLES

LAUNCH PAD WITH ERECTOR

CHERRY PICKER

LAUNCH PAD WITH ERECTOR

MISSILE READY BLDGS

FUELING VEHICLES

23. A U.S. reconnaissance photo of the Cuban missile sites.

that Fidel Castro was friendly towards them, the Russians decided to build missile sites on the island and to send rockets there. The Americans were alarmed. Cuba lay within easy reach of the Southern coastline of the United States, whose cities could now be easily attacked and devastated by the latest weapons of war. The President warned his people of what was happening:

Good evening, my fellow citizens. This government, as promised, has maintained the closest surveillance of the Soviet military build-up on the island of Cuba. Within the past week, unmistakable evidence has established the fact that a series of offensive missile sites is now in preparation on that imprisoned island ... To halt this offensive build-up, a strict quarantine on all offensive military equipment under shipment to Cuba is being initiated ... [13]

The Russians were told that shipping approaching Cuba would be stopped and searched. Any vessels carrying missiles would be turned back. The President was determined not to give in on this issue. He left his opponents a way out by allowing them to withdraw rockets which had already been taken in. The Russians gave in. Kennedy's firmness and good sense won a great victory without any blood being shed.

24. *The old alliance: Kennedy with the British Prime Minister, Harold Macmillan.*

25. *Support for Western Europe: Kennedy with the West German Chancellor, Adenauer.*

26. *A thaw in the Cold War? Kennedy with Kruschev in Vienna in 1961.*

When he travelled abroad, he was always given a good reception by the crowds which came to see him. To them the young-looking Kennedy stood for plain speaking and straight dealing. One of the President's finest moments came in June 1963. Then, he visited Western Germany and went to West Berlin. He reminded the inhabitants that they were not forgotten by other people:

. . . When all are free, then we can look forward to that day

27. In many ways Kennedy was more popular outside than inside the United States; here he receives a warm welcome during a visit to Ireland.

when this city will be joined as one – and this country, and this great continent of Europe – in a peaceful and hopeful glow. When that day finally comes, as it will, the people of West Berlin can take sober satisfaction in the fact that they were in the front lines for almost two decades.

All free men, wherever they may live, are citizens of Berlin, and, therefore, as a free man, I take pride in the words, 'Ich bin ein Berliner'[14]

In August 1963 an agreement was signed by the U.S.S.R., the U.S.A. and Great Britain, banning the testing of nuclear bombs in outer space, in the air and under the sea. Kennedy felt that a definite step had been taken towards creating a more peaceful atmosphere in the world. He had seen the danger to mankind of the immense nuclear power possessed by Russia and the U.S.A. In a speech to the United Nations he had said:

Never have the nations of the world had so much to lose or so much to gain. Together we shall save our planet or together we shall perish in its flames. Save it we can, and save it we must, and then shall we earn the eternal thanks of mankind . . .[15]

28. *The Kennedys set out on the last drive through Dallas, Texas.*

Then in November 1963 President Kennedy visited Texas on a political tour. On 22nd November, with his wife, he went to the city of Dallas. At 11.50 a.m. he entered a large open car in which he was to drive through crowds in the streets. In front of the President and Mrs Kennedy sat Governor Connally of Texas and his wife. Forty minutes later, as the car approached an underpass, Mrs Connally turned to the President and smilingly said: 'You can't say that Texas isn't friendly to you today.' At that moment Kennedy was hit by a shot from behind:

The President was wounded, but not fatally. A 6.5 millimetre bullet had entered the back of his neck, bruised his right lung, ripped his windpipe, and exited at his throat, nicking the knot of his tie. Continuing its flight, it had passed through Governor Connally's back, chest, right wrist, and left thigh . . . [16]

Then a second bullet hit him. His wife cradled his head in her lap as the car roared out of the procession and hurtled towards a nearby hospital. The scene, with a man dying, the inside of the car covered with blood, the confusion and dismay of the onlookers, brought horror to the world when it learned the story.

Kennedy was killed in his prime. No one has been able to

29. *Kennedy's funeral cortege passes through Washington.*

30. *Senator Edward Kennedy, the last survivor of the Kennedy brothers at John's graveside.*

offer any satisfactory explanation of why he was killed. There has been some argument about how he was killed. The man who apparently fired the shots, Lee Harvey Oswald, was himself murdered before deeper investigations could be made.

In his life Kennedy had shown powers of character which brought him the admiration and respect of statesmen from many other nations. He was buried in Arlington National Cemetery and was mourned by people the world over.

Date Line

Here are some dates of importance in the lives of the two Presidents. In your opinion, which others should be added?

Roosevelt
1882 – Born 30th January
1900 – Entered Harvard University
1910 – Elected as Democratic Senator
1913 – Became Assistant Secretary to the Navy
1920 – Stood for Vice-Presidency, defeated
1921 – Infantile paralysis
1928 – Re-entered politics
1932 – Elected President
1936 – Elected for second term
1939 – Second World War
1940 – Elected for third term
1941 – 7th December: Pearl Harbor
1944 – Elected for fourth term
1945 – The Yalta Conference
1945 – Died, 13th April

Kennedy
1917 – Born 29th May
1936 – Entered Harvard University
1937 – Joe Kennedy became U.S. Ambassador in London
1940 – *Why England Slept* published
1941 – Joined U.S. Navy
1943 – Loss of *P.T. 109*
1946 – Entered politics as a Congressman
1952 – Elected Democratic Senator
1953 – Married Jacqueline Bouvier
1956 – *Profiles of Courage* published
     – Stood for Vice-Presidency, defeated
1960 – Elected as President
1961 – Building of Berlin Wall
1962 – The Cuban Crisis
1963 – Assassinated, 22nd November

Glossary

Here is a short glossary which explains some of the names connected with Roosevelt and Kennedy.

The American Constitution: Since 1787, the United States has had a written constitution which marks out the powers of the President and his government and sets out the rights and duties of citizens.

Atlantic Charter, The: Published after a meeting between Roosevelt and Churchill, at sea, in 1941, it listed the freedoms which were to be sought after the war by the democratic powers.

Bay of Pigs, The: The place in Cuba where the ill-fated invasion was made in 1960, in an attempt to overthrow Fidel Castro and his supporters.

Castro, Fidel: A revolutionary whose forces captured control of the government in Cuba. Castro became the leader of a government which sought reforms for all peasants. He has showed friendship towards the Soviet Union but has been on bad terms with the U.S.A.

Congress: A name given to the parliament of the U.S.A. It consists of the Senate and the House of Representatives.

Cuban Crisis, The: An international crisis occurred in 1962 when the Russians began building missile sites in Cuba. The Americans insisted that they should be removed.

Democratic Party: One of America's two large political parties. Both Roosevelt and Kennedy were Democrats.

Eisenhower, Dwight D.: A famous American soldier of the Second World War who later became President of the U.S.A., 1952–60. He was a Republican.

F.B.I.: The American Federal Bureau of Investigation is a form of detective police force. One of their tasks is to protect political leaders.

Fireside Chats: Franklin D. Roosevelt introduced the idea of evening radio talks to the American people, explaining his policies.

Great Slump, or Great Depression: A great slackening of production and trade which began in the U.S.A. and affected many countries of the world after 1929. It led to massive unemployment.

Hot Line, The: A direct telephone link between the White House, Washington and the Kremlin, Moscow, to enable leaders to speak to each other in cases of international emergencies.

Hoover, Herbert: A Republican who was President of the U.S.A. but was defeated by Roosevelt in the 1932 campaign.

House of Representatives: A part of the U.S. parliament. Its members are representatives of various states and stand for election every two years.

Isolationism: This idea was popular with many Americans between the two world wars. It held that the U.S.A. should not become involved by pacts and alliances, with the affairs of other countries.

Johnson, Lyndon B.: The Democratic Vice-President who suddenly had the position of President thrust upon him when Kennedy was assassinated in 1963. He remained in office until 1968.

Kennedy, Jacqueline: As Jacqueline Bouvier, she married John Kennedy in 1953. They had two children, Caroline and John. Mrs Kennedy became a popular figure for her charm and elegance. In 1968 she re-married.

Kennedy, Joseph: Father of some remarkable sons. He himself made a fortune in business and was the U.S. Ambassador to Britain from 1937 to 1940.

Kennedy, Robert: Younger brother of John, he became Attorney-General in the Kennedy administration after 1960. He was shot and killed by an assassin at an election meeting after he had decided to stand for the Presidency in 1968.

Kruschev, Nikita: After the death of Stalin in 1953, Kruschev emerged as the most powerful of his successors. He stayed in power for some years as leader of Russia.

Lease-Lend: The system by which the Roosevelt administration sold, lent and gave vital supplies to Britain during the Second World War.

Missiles: The name given to rockets, often carrying atomic warheads, which have been developed as long range weapons by the U.S.A. and the U.S.S.R. since 1945.

New Deal, The: The scheme introduced by Roosevelt after 1933, which successfully set out to bring work to millions of unemployed Americans who were suffering from the effects of the Great Slump.

New Frontier, The: The name given to the aims of the Kennedy administration after 1960, in bringing social reform and international peace to the U.S.A.

Oswald, Lee Harvey: The assassin of Kennedy. He himself was later shot by Jack Ruby in Dallas.

Party Convention: Both of the large American political parties hold meetings or conventions, where delegates choose candidates who will contest Presidential elections.

Pearl Harbor: An American naval base in Hawaii. The Japanese made an unheralded attack on the U.S. Pacific Fleet, which was moored there on 7th December 1941. This act brought the U.S.A. into the Second World War.

Presidential Election: An election for the office of President of the U.S.A. takes place once every four years.

Republican Party: One of America's two large political parties. It tends to be more conservative than the Democratic Party.

Roosevelt, Eleanor: Wife of Franklin D. Roosevelt, she was a woman of remarkable energy and ability. Her travels took her to many parts of the world.

Roosevelt, Theodore: 'Teddy' Roosevelt was President of the United States in the early years of the present century. He was a remarkable man, full of driving energy.

Ruby, Jack: A citizen of Dallas who shot Lee Harvey Oswald while he was in police custody. Ruby was arrested but died later.

Senator: A member of the U.S. Senate. Each state returns two members to the Senate.

Summit Meeting: The name given to a meeting held between the heads of state of the U.S.S.R. and the U.S.A. The description was applied to Kennedy's talks with Kruschev in 1962.

Tennessee Valley Authority: A giant scheme set up by the Roosevelt administration in the 1930's to bring work and prosperity to a large area of the Southern states. It was part of the New Deal.

Wall Street Crash, The: Shares were sold in panic when the Great Slump came to the U.S.A. The worst period occurred in October 1929, when millions of shares were sold in the Stock Exchange on Wall Street and many people were ruined.

White House, The: The official home of the President of the U.S.A. The house is situated in Washington.

Wilson, Woodrow: The President of the United States at the end of the First World War. He set out Fourteen Points for peace and attended the Treaty of Versailles.

Yalta Conference: A conference held at Yalta, in Russia, towards the end of the Second World War. Roosevelt, Stalin and Churchill made plans for the division of Europe.

Questions

Here are 14 questions for you to attempt. They can be answered in writing or some will make useful starting points for discussion. Which other questions should be asked, in your opinion, to gain a better insight into the Presidents' lives?

1. Where there any similarities between the backgrounds and early lives of Roosevelt and Kennedy?
2. What part did the United States play in the First World War?
3. Why did the United States have a boom in trade during the 1920's?
4. How did Roosevelt overcome his attack of paralysis?
5. What was the 'New Deal'? Why did some Americans oppose it?
6. What were Roosevelt's achievements for his country?
7. Compare the work and powers of an American President with those of an English monarch.
8. Why was Kennedy such a popular figure with the people of many nations?
9. Why is the work of a President's wife so important to his career?
10. Why has violence occurred on several occasions in American political life since 1960?
11. Which qualities were shown by Roosevelt and Kennedy when each was President?
12. What similarities and what differences are there between British and American political parties?
13. When was the most successful part of each man's political career?
14. Which was the greatest problem faced by each President?

Further Reading

There have been many books written about the lives of the two men. Those mentioned below contain much interesting material. You may not be able to read the complete book, but a careful study of certain episodes will give you a clearer picture of the Presidents' lives:

1. James MacGregor Burns, *John Kennedy: a Political Profile*
2. Alan Churchill, *The Roosevelts*
3. William Manchester, *The Death of a President*
4. Ed. Alan Nevins, *The Burden and the Glory*
5. Eleanor Roosevelt, *Autobiography*
6. J. Roosevelt and S. Shalett, *Affectionately F.D.R.*
7. Gene Schoor, *Young John Kennedy*
8. Uwe Schwarz, *John Fitzgerald Kennedy, 1917–1963*
9. Hugh Sidey, *John F. Kennedy: Portrait of a President*
10. Richard J. Whalen, *The Founding Father*
11. Frances Wilkins, *President Kennedy*

Sources of the Extracts

Roosevelt

1. From *The Roosevelts*, Alan Churchill, p. 176
2. From *Affectionately F.D.R.*, J. Roosevelt and S. Shalett, p. 29
3. From *The Autobiography of Eleanor Roosevelt*, p. 45
4. From *The Roosevelts*, p. 219
5. From *Affectionately F.D.R.*, p. 14
6. *Ibid.*, p. 144
7. From 'The Roosevelt Revolution of 1933–38', by Esmond Wright, *History Today*, Dec 1962.
8. From a speech by Herbert Hoover, New York City, 22nd Oct 1928
9. From a letter of F. D. Roosevelt, quoted in *The Roosevelts*, p. 287
10. From *America in the Twentieth Century*, D. K. Adams
11. From *The American Red Cross: a History*, F. R. Dulles
12. From the Roosevelt campaign address, Detroit, 2nd Oct 1932
13. From a speech of F. D. Roosevelt
14. From the Constitution of the U.S.A., Article II, Section I
15. From Roosevelt's First Inaugural Address, 4th Mar 1933
16. From *The Autobiography of Eleanor Roosevelt*, p. 128
17. From Roosevelt's address to the Democratic States Convention, Syracuse, New York, 29th Sept 1936
18. From Harold Ickes, Secretary of the Interior, 1936
19. From *The Autobiography of Eleanor Roosevelt*
20. *Ibid.*
21. From a Roosevelt Fireside Chat, 29th Dec 1940
22. From Roosevelt's Annual Message to Congress, 6th Jan 1941
23. From a speech made by Winston Churchill to both Houses of the U.S. Congress, 26th Dec 1941
24. From Roosevelt's Annual Message to Congress, January, 1942
25. From *The Roosevelts*, p. 314
26. From *The Autobiography of Eleanor Roosevelt*, p. 212

Kennedy

1. From a report made by W. E. Forster
2. From a writing of Joseph Kennedy
3. From a letter written by John F. Kennedy's house-father at Choate
4. From a letter written by Joseph Kennedy
5. From a letter written by John F. Kennedy
6. From *Why England Slept*, John F. Kennedy
7. From a U.S. Navy citation
8. From a radio talk given by John F. Kennedy
9. From Kennedy's acceptance address made to the Democratic National Convention, 1960
10. From *John F. Kennedy*, Hugh Sidey
11. From a speech made by President Kennedy
12. From a television address made to the American people, 11th June 1963
13. From a television speech made during the Cuban Crisis
14. From a speech made in West Berlin, 26th June 1963
15. From a speech made to the General Assembly of the United Nations
16. From *The Death of a President*, William Manchester

Acknowledgements

The following have given permission for the reproduction of photographs: United Press: Figs. 5, 17, 18, 19, 20, 24, 26, 28, 29, 30; The U.S. Information Service: Figs. 1, 2, 12, 15, 16, 23; Keystone Press Agency: Figs. 3, 8, 9, 10, 13, 25, 27; Associated Press: Figs. 4, 11; Radio Times Hulton Picture Library: Fig. 14; Camera Press: Fig. 22;